Why, O Lord?

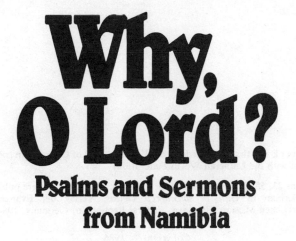

Why, O Lord?

Psalms and Sermons
from Namibia

Zephania Kameeta

Fortress Press   Philadelphia

This book was first published by the World Council of Churches in collaboration with the Lutheran World Federation.

Psalms 23, 55, 62, 68, 69, 115, 126, 127, 133, 137, and 139 were published in German in *Gott in schwarzen Gettos,* Verlag der Evangelisch-Lutherischen Mission, Erlangen, Federal Republic of Germany, 1984.

Library of Congress Cataloging-in-Publication Data

Kameeta, Zephania.
  Why, O Lord?

  1. Bible. O.T. Psalms—Paraphrases, English.
2. Race relations—Religious aspects—Christianity.
3. Namibia—Race relations. 4. Liberation theology.
I. Title.
BS1440.K33 1987   261.8'3489688   86-9856
ISBN 0-8006-1923-4

2541D86 Printed in the United States of America 1-1923

Contents

Introduction

A young fourth-year seminarian sat quietly in his chair, glancing at the clock. It was nearly 11. He raised his hand and asked the lecturer if the class could be excused to listen to the radio. Permission granted, the class hurried towards the radio. It was 21 June 1971. A judge from Pakistan delivered his verdict in an hour-and-a-half broadcast. The judge overturned a 1950 International Court of Justice ruling that South Africa's mandate in Namibia (once South-West Africa) was legal. Now, the court ruled, South Africa was illegally occupying the territory.

Excited, the seminarians returned to their class after the broadcast. A Finnish New Testament professor was lecturing on Romans 13: "Let every soul be subject unto the higher powers. For there is no power but of God: the powers that be are ordained of God..."

The young theology student was Zephania Kameeta. And he remembered later:

> The broadcast raised our hopes so much. After that we accidentally had the New Testament lecture. No, maybe the Lord himself asked the professor on that day to discuss that particular passage.
>
> All authority has been given by God. And you know in South Africa and Namibia this text is the basis of racial separateness — apartheid — and I don't believe in it. Apartheid is not based on a political ideology, but it is based on religion. And this text is one that is being used in South Africa to justify apartheid. Those who are fighting against that, those who are saying things against that — they must be communists or Marxists. That's the attitude.
>
> After we discussed Romans 13, following the World Court decision, we started for the first time to look at the text within the context of this Southern African situation. And we asked our professor within the context of what we heard a few minutes before what he thought was the rule for the church in this kind of situation. Because we read this text (v. 3) where it suggests that authorities are entitled to punish those who are doing wrong and reward those who are doing good.
>
> But our experience up to that day in Namibia was that the authority was there to punish those who are doing good and to praise those who are doing wrong. And we asked: What's the responsibility of the church in this kind of situation? Has the church anything to say? Should the church only be concerned about what is to come? Or should the church be the first-taste of the kingdom of God? Should the church keep quiet in view of the suffering of the people, in view of the injustice?

The professor heard the explosion of questions, paused, and then said: "I believe the church has something to say, but I don't know precisely what at this moment."

The students, more excited now, said they'd give the lecturer a chance to think about that point. But they said they'd boycott classes if the church didn't have anything to say.

Kameeta says it was at that moment that the theology students saw clearly that there was no point in being trained "to serve an organization that will be silent in the face of the suffering of their people".

The students stayed out of class for a whole day. It was the first time there had been anything like a boycott. The next day one of the lecturers met with the students and said, "I'd like to ask you a question: Who then is the church? Is it the lecturers? And if it isn't us — if we're not doing or saying anything — then why are you not acting? Why aren't you doing anything?"

The provocative question startled the students. After a brief discussion they decided to draft an open letter to South African Prime Minister B.J. Vorster. The church boards of the two large Lutheran churches in Namibia were meeting at that time. They read the students' letter and decided to accept it. On 30 June 1971, the leaders of the Evangelical Lutheran Ovambokavango Church and the Evangelical Lutheran Church in Namibia/SWA sent the open letter.

In deferential but firm language the letter said the South African government "failed to take cognizance of Human Rights as declared by the UN". The letter demonstrated a growing consciousness and consensus among the country's overwhelming black majority. Writer Heinz Hunke in his book, *Namibia: The Strength of the Powerless*, has said: "No other single document has ever had such an immediate and lasting influence in Namibia as this letter. The black population recognized that their feelings were being expressed by their church leaders.... From now on the neat network of lies and propaganda would be destroyed again and again by the unintimidated denouncements of church leaders who belonged to the oppressed majority."

Namibia — nearly the size of the US states of Texas and Oklahoma together — had become a German territory in 1884. The Germans drove the native black population off their ancestral lands with guns and cannons. In 1906 the Germans nearly exterminated the entire Herero people of central Namibia to quash resistance to their colonial rule. In 1915, during World War I, South African soldiers drove the Germans out of the largely desert territory. And the League of Nations mandated the territory to South Africa in 1920.

Largely because of the rich deposits of copper, diamonds and uranium, South Africa has continued to occupy Namibia long after the World Court and the United Nations ruled that it should give the country its independence. A liberation movement — the South-West Africa People's Organization (SWAPO) — has led the struggle for independence and against the brutal South African occupation. Of the country's 1.2 million people, 70 per cent of whom are Christian, a number have been killed or wounded in the liberation struggle.

Kameeta is now a pastor, and vice-president of his church. The lesson he learned from Romans 13 has animated his life, writings and preaching. He has been attacked by government newspapers; he has witnessed the brutal treatment other church leaders have experienced. "But we are used to these things," he says. "In this kind of situation the church of Christ should be prepared to take up the cross and follow the very same route he took."

He told an interviewer: "Human rights is almost a luxury to us. We are struggling for human lives. People are dying; people are being tortured to death; people are being humiliated every day. That's what people call apartheid." As a pastor he has watched a woman from his congregation's youth group die in his arms after she was refused treatment at both a hospital and a doctor's office. He has had seven funerals for babies in his parish who died in a single week because there was no vaccine available.

Pastor Kameeta once wrote:

> When we declare the good news of our Lord Jesus Christ in Namibia, we experience daily that God leads us in our struggle for liberation and peace. Throughout the history of humanity God has revealed himself as the God of the downtrodden and suffering. God's great act of liberation, the Exodus, constituted the content of life and faith in the history and confession of Israel. The liberating word which God spoke is clearly recognizable throughout the Old Testament — in the story of creation, in the Exodus-event and in

the proclamation of the prophets. This liberating word became flesh and came to live among us in our meaninglessness and our alienation, in our insecurity and our misery, in our pain and our humiliation; it came to liberate us, to lead us out of this ghetto, to call us to peace and to reconciliation with God and with our fellow human beings.

And he described the contents of his writings as "the tears of the suffering people of Namibia, tears wept in our ghettos, on the settlements which are in the possession of whites, in the cities, in the prisons, in the torture chambers and in the 'homelands'".

Through the words of this book, Pastor Kameeta shares with us his faith as he lives in this oppressive situation, and his conviction that, because of God and his Christ, no situation is entirely without hope.

Roger Kahle
Department of Communication
Lutheran World Federation

Why, O Why, Lord

You know, Lord, what is going on, this moment,
in the hearts of Toivo ya Toivo,
Nelson Mandela and Aaron Mushimba.
Certainly you know the hearts of my brethren
their daily sufferings, far away on the vast
and lonely weald, among the sheep.
You see them despised and neglected,
paid a mere trifle; you read their thoughts
deep down in the pits, where they are slaving
for next to nothing.

Lord, the many new graves of the children from Soweto
are well known to you, and so are the tears
of their parents and comrades. You are undeceived
by the reasoning and hypocrisy of Turnhalle;
you have observed the hundreds of prisoners
maltreated in the camps of north Namibia.
They are cruelly struck with the butt-ends of rifles;
cigarettes are put out against their naked bodies.
We are miserable and afflicted like the children
of Israel in Egypt. And you are aware of it all.

Why, O why, Lord?
Why do you seem deaf to our doleful cries?
Or have you turned your back upon us?
How long will you allow them to trample us underfoot?
Is our trust nothing to you, is our hope vain?
Why, why, why do you keep us waiting?

Why, O why, Lord?
Why did you create us? Did you make us only to be shot
like dogs infected with rabies? Did you make us to be
oppressed and put to scorn for ever? Why, Lord, why?
Are there limits to your love, and are we expelled?
Did you make us "Kaffers", "Bantus", "Non-whites"?

Were we doomed to stand humbly at the back door of the
     "Baas",
receiving a splash of water from a rusty marmelade tin?
Did you create us to live on "Yea, Baas" and "yea, Missus"?

1

Did you make us the human caricatures of this world?
Why, O why, Lord, did you create us?

Why, O why, Lord
Why did you tell us through your word that we were made
in your own image? Why this teaching that, regardless of
language,
race and colour, all men are equal in your eyes,
and that we ought to treat and accept each other as such?
Why did you make us realize that our slavery is at an end,
that we are liberated men and women, bought at a high price
with the blood of your only Son? It might have been better
if you had let us alone in our blindness; it would have been
easier then to submit to our fate. It is impossible now.
We have been brought to see, for ourselves,
that we are incomparably more precious than all diamonds
from Oranjemund and all uranium from Rossing.
Why, O why, Lord, did you open our eyes?

Why, O why, Lord?
Why don't you answer when we cry out to you? How long
will you remain passive, looking silently at our agony
and our tears? The yoke has become unendurable,
we won't carry it one step farther.
Why do you allow iniquity and lies to rule over us,
you who redeemed us at the cost of your own life?
You are King of kings and they struck you with their
fists and cudgels; they spat upon you to show their
utter contempt! Cruel nails pierced your hands and feet,
and all this only because of your great and infinite
love for us. Why, O why then are you silent?

From the depths we call to you: Save us in our distress!
Guide us in the right way to Namibia, and not
to a neo-colonial Southwest Africa.
O Lord of the whole world,
refresh our souls and make them new; we are consumed
with thirst for release, righteousness, redemption,
Shalom. Fill our callous, empty hands with your good gifts.
Crush the copper gates and shatter the iron locks

of Robben Island. Break up the prison camps where
our brethren are captive and tortured, help them, Lord!
We call to you, save us in our deadly fear!
We are trembling and feeble. Take our destiny in your
strong right hand; through us let the world see your wonders!
Give us the Spirit of Life so that we may arise.
Then help us to raise, unwearyingly, under your guidance,
the beacons of your kingdom in this country! Amen.

Otjimbingue, 1.9.1976

Mission Theology and
Mission Strategy in Africa

Do we really mean Christian theology?

We speak here of Christian theology; we must state it clearly and unambiguously that our concern here is not the human logos, but the logos of God, which "became a human being and, full of grace and truth, lived among us" (John 1:14). With his life and work, he explained the purpose of his coming into this world: "… the Son of man, did not come to be served, but to serve and to give his life to redeem many people" (Matt. 20:28).

The word of this world enslaves, but the word of God liberates. The word of this world manipulates, dictates, and domesticates, but the word of God is calling us to responsibility and co-responsibility. The word of this world explains itself with imported ideas and slogans, the word of God is revealing itself in participation in the daily sufferings and joys of humanity. The word of God is born of love, while the word of this world is born in egoism and nurtured by hatred.

Let us look at a few examples of the word of this world from the "Christian" Southern Africa:

"Yes, they're inferior in every way."

"Yes, they've just come out of the trees… I mean they're at a lower stage in the evolutionary ladder."

"Blacks have a different attitude to life. They don't believe in hard work."

"On the whole they're stupid… raw. They've got no brains."

"I treat them fairly, but I have my reservations. I can't get myself to want to share a table or anything like that with them."

"They would make pigstys of nice houses."

"They're coming close to being like us. They're getting cheeky, they want to wear fancy clothes and they don't take their hats off when they speak to you anymore." [1]

The word of God is working in and with the liberated one, to transform this evil reality emanating from the human logos. In this revolutionary transformation of the human person and the destructive conditions in which he or she is living, do we hear and see the coming of the kingdom of God?

---

[1] *South African Outlook*, November 1979.

Mission is not a later development, but a dynamic movement of creation and renewal

Mission and creation are not two different aspects in God's salvation history, but a single act of liberation. In the beginning when God created the universe, God sent his word on the mission of creation: "Then God commanded, 'Let there be light' and light appeared... Then God commanded, 'Let there be a dome to divide the water and to keep it in two separate places' — and it was done. Then God commanded, 'Let the earth produce all kinds of animal life'... and it was done. Then God said: 'And now we will make human beings; they will be like us and resemble us. They will have power over the fish, the birds and all animals, domestic and wild, large and small.' So God created human beings, making them to be like himself" (Gen. 1).

The mission of God's liberating word didn't stop on the seventh day, but continued in the redeeming presence of God in the universe. Every page of the Holy Bible witnesses to this mission: "Then the Lord said, 'I have seen how cruelly my people are being treated in Egypt; I have heard them cry out to be rescued from their slave drivers. I have known all about their sufferings, and so I have come down to rescue them... Now I am sending you to the king of Egypt so that you can lead my people out of his country" (Ex. 3). This mission continued in the messages of the prophets. "Then I heard the Lord say, 'Whom shall I send? Who will be our messenger?' I answered 'I will go! Send me!'... He will not judge by appearance or hearsay; he will judge the poor fairly and defend the rights of the helpless... He will rule his people with justice and integrity..." (Isa. 6). "Do not say that you are too young, but go to the people I send you to, and tell them everything I command you to say... Today I give you authority over nations and kingdoms to uproot and to pull down, to destroy and to overthrow, to build and to plant" (Jer. 1).

He created and blessed, but when they turned their backs against his love and truth, he chased them out of the garden. He then gathered them after the flood and opened again the doors of his blessing. When they were oppressed, he led them out of slavery with his mighty hand of liberation. He brought them in the shadow of his blessing, but again when they turned their

backs against his liberating love and truth, he destroyed the
Temple which had become the symbol of the evil status quo,
overthrew their government and sent them into exile. But when
they turned back to him, he didn't hesitate to prepare a road in
the wilderness of despair and to lead them through the doors of
blessing. We witness this divine mission also in the unwritten
pages of the history of God's liberating presence among the
nations of our one world.

The living promise of the rising Sun was from the beginning
present in the mission of the word; and through it we observe in
our faith the clear distinction between the human logos and the
living word of God: "Before the world was created, the word
already existed; he was with God, and he was the same as God.
From the very beginning the word was with God. Through him
God made all things; not one thing in all creation was made
without him. The word was the source of life, and this life
brought light to mankind" (John 1). God fulfilled his promise,
he sent his only Son, the bright dawn of salvation, so that
everyone who believes in him may not die but have eternal life.

The Book of Malachi can be rightly seen as a bridge where-
upon we cross, in our faith, from the Old to the New Covenant:
"But for you who obey me, my saving power will rise on you
like the sun and bring healing like the sun's rays. You will be as
free and happy as calves led out of a stall" (Mal. 4:2).

This Sun rose, not in arrogance, according to the world's
expectations, but in all humility. He became an ordinary
human being and lived among ordinary human beings. The
glory which they saw shone forth from his humility. "He had
no dignity or beauty to make us take notice of him. There was
nothing attractive about him, nothing that would draw us to
him. We rejected him... But because of our sins he was
wounded, beaten because of the evil we did. We are healed by
the punishment he suffered, made whole by the blows he
received... Like a lamb about to be slaughtered... he never
said a word. He was arrested and sentenced and led off to die,
and no one cared about his fate... his death was a sacrifice to
bring forgiveness" (Isa. 53).

He sent his disciples, Paul, Stephen and many others, on this
very same road of suffering and victory. This is the same road
along which he is sending us today in Africa.

In Africa

Africa is a suffering continent, and the sorrow in her heart is so great that it almost crushes her. Distress and anguish are the lot of her children, and their tears are like drops of blood falling to the ground. She is suffering from apartheid, exploitation and neo-colonialism. We will deal with apartheid and exploitation in the Southern Africa context; but allow me to say a few words about neo-colonialism. This tragic phenomenon arises when the oppressed of yesterday — after their victory — become today's oppressors. They forget that the struggle for liberation doesn't end with the day of independence. Instead of serving and giving their lives to redeem the people, they want to be served and worshipped, and even take the lives of their people, so that they can live in luxury. The Lord has chosen his church to be a living witness in such situations, and to proclaim with her existence the new community in him. The world will then see and learn from the church the essence of this community, the new community of the liberated people who belong together in worship and life. The walls of division and animosity will be destroyed and scattered humanity will be gathered from the "first", "second" and "third" worlds into the One World in which God created all of us in his own image.

While the world is being told that the monster of apartheid is dead, it is roaming like a hungry lion and devours the children of Africa. We live under the rule of terror — of arbitrary arrest, indefinite detention, brutal torture and house arrest. We live under the inhuman and uncivilized acts of the South African army in northern Namibia. Hundreds are leaving their homes because of death threats, and are taking refuge in the southern parts of the country. The whole of Namibia is rapidly becoming an "operational area".

Church activities are frequently interrupted, and property destroyed by the "security forces" in northern Namibia. Marriage services, funerals and holy communion services are being interrupted, the participants beaten up and arrested. At the time of writing, a medical doctor serving in our church hospital, the editor of our church magazine and a pastor serving among the workers have been restricted to Windhoek. They must not leave their houses from 18.00 to 6.00 and they are not allowed to meet with more than five people at a time.

As on that day of the Golden Calf, the South African regime and its supporters are dancing around a white calf, possessed by the evil spirit of racial madness. The music behind this dance is provided by the false prophets and betrayers of the Lord Jesus Christ. Their songs and prayers adore the white calf, their congregations are in reality racial clubs, and they work day and night for the destruction of the new community in Christ.

Those who refuse to partake in this dance and who are working for the destruction of the white calf, are served with the "Nacht und Nubel" decrees. The only "peaceful" and "democratic" way allowed "to solve the problem" is to join in the dance around the white calf.

The "Tale of Two Migrants" gives us a glimpse of one aspect of the destructive result of this dance of hell:

> Mr Vusi Zwane lives in a hostel room in Soweto with five other men. He sees his family once a year in Gazankulu. He is a carpenter, but his job is to empty dustbins in the white suburbs of Johannesburg. Mr Peter Smith, his wife and three kids live in their own five-roomed house in Kempton Park. Mr Smith is also a carpenter and has a permanent job with a building contractor. Smith and Zwane are both skilled workers. The difference is that Smith is a British immigrant and Zwane is a black migrant worker. The Government's proposed new deal for skilled immigrants accentuates the inequalities between the Smiths and Zwanes of South Africa. These inequalities dominate every sphere of life.

> **Getting in**
> *Mr Smith* applies for immigrant status from Bradford, England. Because he is a trained carpenter, and the building industry is in short supply of such skills, he doesn't need a firm job offer. This is one of the features of the new immigrant deal. He fills out the necessary papers and waits to be accepted. With the new deal he is not likely to wait more than three months.

> *Mr Zwane* registers at his local labour bureau as a skilled carpenter. He must wait until a recruitment officer offers him a suitable position. Although there is a large building operation in the nearest town, there are no jobs available. No job offers come from Johannesburg, as officials say there are enough skilled workers in the city. Mr Zwane waits for eight months. In desperation he travels to Jo'burg without the necessary papers and finds his own job on a building site. On registering at Albert Street the next day he is endorsed out. He goes back to Gazankulu, registered as an unskilled worker, and gets a one-year contract to empty dustbins.

Travel

Once the Smiths have been accepted as immigrants they will come to South Africa on a government assisted passage. At present the government pays R.275 per person, but the new deal says this is likely to go up to R.500.

Mr Zwane's employer is supposed to pay his travel costs from Gazankulu to Jo'burg, but Mr Zwane never sees the money.

The good life

When the Smiths arrive in South Africa they will be given free board and lodging until they find themselves a home. With the help of the government or his employer, Smith may raise a housing loan in less than a week. A month later the Smiths' children may have settled in a good school to which their mother takes them daily in her new Golf.

Mr Zwane will have to live in the hostel accommodation found for him by his employer. His family will need special permission to come from Gazankulu for a visit.

Citizenship

Mr Smith and his family are happy to be here, and want to become SA citizens. The Smiths apply for permanent residence which, with the new deal, is likely to be given after two years. Later the Smiths will have the vote and the political power that comes with it.

Mr Zwane would like to live permanently with his family in Soweto. But he is a migrant labourer with only Section 10.1(d) rights. He cannot earn the right to become an urban dweller as he is on a yearly contract. If his homeland becomes independent he will lose his South African citizenship altogether.

Job security

With a work permit, Mr Smith is free to accept or reject jobs as he finds them. If he is retrenched he may seek alternative employment. While unemployed, Smith can draw UIF which will be 45% of his previous monthly earnings if he has been employed for 25 weeks that year.

Mr Zwane's contract lasts one year, and binds him to a particular job. At the end of the year he depends on his employer's decision to renew the contract. Mr Zwane may collect UIF benefits, but only in the homelands, and this may take months. [2]

---

[2] *Sunday Post*, 27 January 1980.

The dance around the white calf continues, and the rights of millions are being offered as sacrifices to this god: the right to life, liberty, security and peace, the right to food, clothing, housing, sufficient health care, rest and leisure, the right to freedom of expression, education and culture, the right to freedom of thought, conscience and religion, the right to work and adequate working conditions and a just wage, the right of assembly and association, the right to freedom of movement, the right to be a human being created in the image of God.

"Go, then, to all peoples everywhere and make them my disciples..."

That must be our strategy: to forego the luxury of developing abstract concepts and using the obscure language of theological experts; to go to all people everywhere and proclaim with your whole being the presence and coming of the kingdom of God.

To be equipped with the Holy Spirit of unity and power so that you will be able to stand up against the evil structures of racism, oppression and exploitation. For we are not fighting against human beings but against the wicked "Super Powers" of this dark age. So stand up from the conference tables and put on God's armour now! Then, in this evil day, you will be able to resist the enemy's attacks; and after fighting to the end, you will still hold your ground.

So stand ready, with truth as a belt tight around your waist in the midst of their lies on the radio, television, newspapers, education systems, racially oriented parliaments and pulpits.

Stand ready with righteousness as your breastplate in the midst of the army of unrighteousness; and as your shoes the readiness to announce the good news of peace. At all times hold on to the Lord Jesus Christ, and victory will be yours in the struggle. And accept liberation as a helmet in the heat of contempt and slavery. Take the word of God as the sword which the Spirit gives you.

Do all this in prayer, asking for God's help. Pray on every occasion and everywhere as the Spirit leads. Keep alert and never give up; pray always for the new community and all God's people in our one world. And pray also for the confessing church in South Africa and Namibia, so that it may speak boldly and make known the secret of the gospel.

A Black Theology of Liberation

It is the word "black" which repeatedly raises questions. And there is usually a great fear behind these questions. One may speak of "European" theology, "American" theology, "Calvinist" theology, "Lutheran" theology, or even "white" theology. But as soon as you couple "black" with theology, suspicion and fear are aroused, leading to persecution and violence. That is something which happens not only when "black" and "theology" are joined, but also when "black" is associated with "power", or when "black" is associated with "consciousness". What is the magic in this word?

"Black" is a word which, like a mirror, reflects indescribable wretchedness. It is not a philosophical concept or an ideology or a colour; one sees in it the masses of oppressed humanity. It evokes the black reality in conflict with the status quo. Through this word the reality in which the oppressed live day and night is brought before the oppressors and their tremendous machinery of violence.

In summary, then, the word "black" does not mean a certain colour, but a condition of wretchedness in which the oppressed live. It is this condition which is being made relevant to the word of God.

God speaks a liberating word

God is essentially free. Nothing and nobody can push God around. And in freedom God created the world, a free creation. Let me emphasize this: not only Europe was created to be free, but the whole cosmos of which Southern Africa is a part. As God in his holiness is free, so God's actions in the history of this world are actions for liberation.

The cry for freedom does not just resonate through humanity and nature. It is also God's own cry, for our God identifies himself with his people and his creation. The groans of his Spirit can be heard in the groans of the starving, his Spirit agonizes in the agony of the imprisoned and suffers silently in the mute suffering of nature. Our God is not an apathetic God who, satisfied and pleased with himself, now complacently sleeps in heaven. On the contrary, he is a compassionate God who suffers with us precisely because he loves. His spirit suffers with his people in the exile, in the ghetto and in the throes of persecution. He suffers with his enslaved creation. Because God created nature as a game of his love for joy,

11

his Spirit is moved by the long history of suffering in the world and participates in this suffering. His spirit too hungers and cries for freedom. [1]

If God is free by nature, and if God longs that we be free, how can the word that he speaks be anything but the message of liberation? God does not speak this word into a vacuum, but into the situation of hunger and poverty, the situation in which people are systematically destroyed by racial discrimination and electric shocks, in locations and compounds, and the conditions created by barbaric and inhuman laws and regulations, the pass laws, the immorality laws, group areas laws and so on. Into, and from, this situation the Lord speaks the liberating word, the black theology of liberation. It is this word which is welcomed as "glad tidings" by those who suffer but which is regarded by the oppressors as dangerous communist propaganda. This word confronts the status quo, liberates the oppressed and works revolutionary changes. This word is not philosophical and abstract as those who maintain the status quo would want it, but it is the word which was born in poverty, on hard stone. It is Jesus the Liberator whose voice speaks with urgency to "Christian" Southern Africa.

The reality of sin

When evil practices take root and grow within a community, it is never by chance, it is because people opt for them. Not necessarily atheists or people who stand outside the church, but those people who claim that they are Christians and that they are acting according to Christian principles.

Sin is not just something which can be confined to individuals; it is also clearly to be discerned in the history of communities. Sin is not just an individual, personal, private or inner reality; it is a destructive reality within the structures and systems of our community. It is a visible reality which can only be countered by a visible liberation. Sin is a socio-political and historical fact. Sin is there where people are oppressed and exploited, where people are governed by violence, where people are deprived of their rights. Sin can only be confronted

---

[1] Jurgen Moltmann, *Freedom in the Light of Hope.*

and destroyed by the actual, revolutionary word of liberation. Only this liberating word of Yahweh can free and save people from oppressive structures. But this liberation is a gift of God to humanity in bondage. Through the death and resurrection of his Son, God has healed the broken relationship between himself and humankind.

Those who are liberated are not liberated just for themselves, but they are used as instruments of liberation in this world. Those who have really tasted this liberation do not withdraw into a "spiritual" sphere, but they go into the world and sacrifice themselves for the liberation of their neighbours. They go out as bearers of good news to the poisoned community. With this message of liberation they confront the reality of sin within the ungodly structures. Thus one is here not talking of ministers who interfere in politics; it is basically a matter of choosing between justice and injustice, between liberation and slavery and oppression. Here in Southern Africa we are not concerned with the church and the state, but with the struggle between Christ and the powers of evil.

It is the calling of the church to be involved in this struggle. Everyone who calls himself or herself a Christian is called to this struggle. It is a command from Christ. To uphold it the Lutheran churches in Southern Africa issued the following statement:

> To us the political system now prevailing in the RSA appears to be based on a number of misapprehensions and errors. We are convinced that this whole system needs to be radically reconsidered and reappraised in the light of the biblical revelation and of the general experience of mankind. We affirm that a political system can be accepted as valid only insofar as it does not obstruct the will and purpose of God. We affirm that the political system in force in South Africa, with its discrimination against some sectors of the population, its acceptance of the break-up of many families, its concentration of power in the hands of one race only, and the limitations it imposes on freedom, cannot be reconciled with the gospel of the grace of God in Jesus Christ.
>
> We affirm that this system in many ways hinders the exercise of Christian fellowship.
>
> We affirm that it is the duty of all Christian citizens of South Africa to study this system carefully and to work out definite and practical proposals by which it can be changed. Christians are

peacemakers. They are not cowardly pacifists, but they are pacifists who are sent out into the storm in order to change, in a non-violent struggle, oppressive structures and conditions. We are aware that... the righteousness God has given to us becomes the criterion of our personal and social relationships. We are also aware that those who accept racial divisions as guiding principles in the life and organization of our churches, and those who countenance the deprivation of human rights, dignity and worth of people created in the image of God, exclude themselves from the fellowship of Christian believers. [2]

Jesus Christ is the liberator of the whole of humanity. In him there is no discrimination. It is blasphemous for South Africa to claim that it is a Christian country while it deprives the black people of their God-given freedom and dignity because of their colour. In the new, liberated community one's neighbours cannot be economically exploited, politically oppressed and deprived of their social rights; but all these are shared with them in love.

The black theology of liberation challenges every Christian in Southern Africa to take this step, the first towards liberation, reconciliation, peace and justice. Deep wounds will result, but it is the only way, the way of the cross. That is the way of hope and victory.

---

[2] FELKSA Conference, 11-13 February 1975.

Mary's Song of Praise
Luke 1:46–55

Today I look into my own heart
and all around me, and I sing the song of Mary.

My life praises the Lord my God
who is setting me free.
He has remembered me, in my humiliation and distress!
From now on those who rejected and ignored me
will see me and call me happy,
because of the great things he is doing
in my humble life.
His name is completely different from the other names in this
    world;
    from one generation to another,
    he was on the side of the oppressed.
As on the day of the Exodus, he is stretching out
his mighty arm to scatter the oppressors
with all their evil plans.
He has brought down mighty kings
from their thrones
and he has lifted up the despised;
and so will he do today.
He has filled the exploited with good things,
and sent the exploiters away with empty hands;
and so will he do today.
His promise to our mothers and fathers remains new and fresh to
    this day.
Therefore the hope for liberation
which is burning in me
will not be extinguished.
He will remember me, here now and beyond the grave.

A Christmas Meditation
Isaiah 9:2–6

The people of Namibia who are living under daily oppression and dehumanization are now seeing a bright light of hope in the holy child who humbly comes to live among them.

The light of the good news of liberation is shining upon them, and gives them new strength to resist the evil of compulsory military service in a foreign army of oppression.

O Lord, you are giving them great joy in the midst of danger and fear; in faith they know that you are particularly near to your people in all such situations.

Your presence gives them joy in this dark hour in the history of their land. They are grateful that you are holding their trembling hands in your strong hand.

As you in ages past saw the suffering and fears of your people and came to liberate them from oppression and hatred, so are you coming today to do the same for us. Your coming cannot be prevented by military might. Our enemies are powerful, but you are God, the Almighty. It is in this confidence that we confess your liberating name in the midst of death.

For unto us a child is born, here in our suffering. Unto us a son is given, here in our fear and despair. He is King above all the lords. His name is holy and shall be called:

Wonderful — for he spoke only a word and this wonderful creation came into being. He made it all in his wisdom and love. He created humanity in his image, all people equal in his sight.

His majesty is above the highest heavens, but yet he gave it all up, took upon him the life of a servant and lived among us.

He took from me the crown of thorns and gave me his crown of righteousness. He went down to hell so that I may be with him in heaven.

Counseller — he leads us daily with his word from a situation of not knowing what decision to take. As he did in the past, he is leading us from despair into hope. And when they bring us before governers and kings for his sake, we shall not be worried of what we shall speak, for it will be given to us by his Spirit of power, wisdom, and love.

The mighty God — who is doing great things in our lives. He has scattered the proud with their plans and put down the mighty from their seats. But he is giving honour to the lowly ones. He is filling the hungry with good things and sends the rich empty away.

When we think that it is now the end, for him it is the beginning of big events. When it is completely dark in our lives, his presence shines on as the star of Bethlehem, leading us to the manger to see and experience the great things which the Lord is doing among his people.

The everlasting Father — who is the beginning and also the end. He was from the beginning, is now and will come again in his glory. He cannot be compared with anyone else, for there is no one who is like him. He is God forever. He does not become tired or weak. Those who wait upon him receive new strength, and they will persist in the struggle without becoming tired. Those who are threatening us daily and even take our lives so that the lie may prosper will not remain forever.

For to him alone belongs the kingdom, the power and the glory, for ever and ever.

The Prince of Peace — that peace which is completely different from the peace which is being enforced upon us with destructive weapons.

He is the King who is opening the doors bolted with fear, with his victorious shalom.

He is sending us into the world with this shalom, to liberate humanity from fear, to break down the walls of division and animosity and to proclaim visibly the reconciliation for which he died on the cross.

He will let his light of hope shine on all who are sitting in the darkness of despair and in the shadow of death.

And even if I die today, that will not prevent the rising of the sun tomorrow. Our hope in our Lord is greater than the fear of death.

For God loved us so dearly and embraced us with his Son, our liberator, whom he sent into our suffering, so that he could shine like the sun in all his glory and expel the night of despair, fear and death.

Zachariah's Prophecy
Luke 1:68–79

Let us not forget our Lord
who is holding the whole world in his hands,
the God of Namibia!
He has come to the help of those
who cried for freedom.
The liberation of which we hoped
and dreamed has become a reality through Jesus Christ, his Son.
Together with him we will break the chains of slavery
and break down the walls of separation.
In the footsteps of the prophets and martyrs we will confront,
with the confession of God's love,
the powers of hatred and destruction in this world.
Our strength is his promise to rescue us from those who want to
    destroy us.
Under his protection, fear will disappear from our lives,
so that we might be faithful before him all the days of our life.

You, my Lord, will be my God
in all my words and deeds,
in my whole life.

In this work, O Lord, as your servant,
go ahead of me and prepare for me the road.
Give me the courage to proclaim
your liberation and forgiveness.
Make me merciful and compassionate as you are.
Let the bright dawn of liberation rise
on me and on all those who live
in the dark shadows of slavery and oppression.
Guide our steps into the path of justice and peace.

An Easter Sermon

My God, my God, why hast thou forsaken me?
As the world sees it, this is the greatest tragedy of all time. Listen to the mocking shouts directed at the one on the cross. Come down from the cross and save yourself!... He saved others, but he cannot save himself... King of Israel, indeed! Let him come down from the cross, then we will believe him!

The cross of Golgotha is in the eyes of the world a sign of defeat and scandal. It is impossible for the world to believe that the Son of God the almighty could hang from such a shameful pole. He ought to be living in a magnificent and well-defended palace. He should have a defence budget of millions of Rands, with which to purchase the most modern military weapons available and train the mightiest of armies. And his person should be guarded day and night by his soldiers. Indeed his power should be so great that, if need be, he could declare truth to be a lie, and lies as truth, acts of love as acts of violence, and acts of violence as acts of love. He should have enough power to persuade God to change his mind.

In the eyes of the world, this man on the cross is a deceiver and a blasphemer, a threat to law and order. He is a weakling trying to assume the position and power of a king. But he doesn't have what it takes.

In the face of all that the world requires of those who wield power, Jesus cries out from the cross in a loud voice: My God, my God, why hast thou forsaken me?

The apostles of "law" and "order", the protectors of Israel's identity, race and culture, hear in this cry an acknowledgment of defeat and despair. It is a confirmation of what they think of this man: a complete failure. But for those who yearn for liberation from the cruel clutches of the evil powers of this world it is the triumphant shout of a victorious hero! God be praised, he did not carry out only half of Yahweh's commission to liberate the world, but he steadfastly went on to its completion, even to the cross. God be praised, he did not get down from the cross, he did not leave the field before the decisive battle could be fought. But he stood firm until he had won the victory and so confirmed

---

• The sermon was preached at a meeting of the Namibia National Convention on Easter Sunday, 1976. (This is a translation of the original Afrikaans text.)

19

once and for ever the reality of God's liberating will in this world! God be praised for leaving him there to accept me. He himself went through hell to bring me out of there.

May the name of the Lord be praised because this cry of Jesus Christ is the fulfilment of God's promise of salvation. Each punch in the face, each mocking word, each blow of the hammer mercilessly driving the nails through his hands was a determined step towards the goal, the liberation of the world! Suffering was not in itself his aim, which was the liberation of the whole creation and the establishment of God's rule in this world. That is the rule of justice, truth and peace. Not that peace which is imposed upon people by armoured cars, batons, guns and police dogs, but that peace which, like a clear stream, flows from the inexhaustible spring of God's love, from self-surrender and service to God and neighbour.

Those who love this truth, justice and peace, follow these determined footsteps of Christ to liberation. Each restriction or banishment which they endure, each cuff or kick, each day in the cells of loneliness, each electric shock, each barbaric indignity suffered by a prisoner to make him or her give false evidence against companions in the struggle, each humiliation met on the roads (for instance when women are examined by male so-called officials), each one who dies of beatings, each tear shed in this fight against evil, for the sake of peace, truth and justice, is a determined step forward in the footsteps of our Hero and Victor. Through all these acts of oppression the structure of repression places itself under the judgment of God. All those deeds done in the hope of self-preservation are deeds of self-destruction.

The tension of this battle here on Golgotha is so great that it takes one's breath away. The revolution which it brings about is incomparable; it is deep and comprehensive.

The events of Golgotha take place in the midst of a crowd which cries out, "Crucify him! Crucify him!"; they take place in this world which hates the truth and prefers the lie, rejects unity and chooses division.

The events of Golgotha shake the foundations of my life. Its violence is so great that nothing and nobody can be unaffected by it. The Roman officer, whose responsibility it was to see that all went smoothly with the crucifixion, was so struck by the violence of the cross that he totally forgot his armoured cars, his guns and dogs. He was only aware of this liberating violence of the cross. And he could do no other than call out, "Truly this was a son of God." It is true, as this man said, he *was* the Son of God; and he is the Son of God *today*, and he will be the Son of God to all eternity. This man was the very first witness; he was not afraid to testify to what he had experienced, in front of the mocking crowd.

The repercussions of the battle of Golgotha were felt not only by those who stood around the cross or by those who stood in the temple, but by the whole creation. God's promise to free the whole creation was being fulfilled. For three hours the light of the sun was withheld. Nature, which had been defiled by evil, was now caught up in the liberating purposes of God, and recreated by the cross. Those who forbid me to proclaim this gospel of the re-created creation of God, who wish to chain me to the altar and pulpit, those are the ones who would banish God from God's own creation! Nature is also liberated by the blood of Jesus Christ, and those who exploit it to the advantage of a particular race and colour at the expense of all others, those who use some people because of their race and colour as slaves to extract the riches of nature for their own benefit, place themselves directly under the judgment of God.

The curtain which is spoken of here separated the holy of holies from the sanctuary. Only the high priest, once a year, was allowed to go in there, bearing an offering. The Evangelist reports that the curtain that served as a division between these two places was torn in two, from top to bottom. Heaven and earth are reconciled to each other! Through Christ, God has made peace with us. Now we no longer need a special person to intercede for us once a year through an offering, because heaven and earth have been reconciled to each other through Jesus Christ. We can now go to God through Christ at any time. The wall of enmity, which we ourselves erected between God and ourselves, has been pulled down by the violence of the cross.

But that is not all. There are other consequences. The wall between race and race, between colour and colour, has been pulled down. In this lies the revolution of the cross. This is the deep and all-embracing revolution. It is inclusive in the sense that it is not restricted to the altar or pulpit, but extends through the history of this world, through the powers and structures of injustice, oppression and exploitation. Every system and government which builds up these separating walls between people and people stands in direct confrontation with the revolution of the cross! This revolution goes deep, in the sense that it converts the heart, the whole personality of the person. And those who are so converted are used by God as instruments of liberation — to cast down the powers, structures and governments which build these walls between people and people and between people and God, by the word of the cross, the sword of the Spirit.

Dear friends, this is what the gospel is about. It tells us what God has done to us through Jesus Christ. Our guilt is washed away if we believe in him. The gospel calls us to conversion. And conversion is a painful process, an indescribable challenge. In this conversion I am torn free of the lie, injustice, hatred, exploitation and the oppression of my fellow men and women. I am freed from racism. This tearing free leaves bleeding wounds behind. That is why we fear conversion. That is why we flee from the face of God and God's word. Facing that challenge, one may even go so far as to defend oneself with all that one has at one's disposal, to defend the evil in which one is caught up with automatic weapons, dogs and batons. And worse than that, one can go so far as to create a god who favours lies, injustice, hatred, exploitation, oppression and the separation of people. And those who oppose this god are looked upon as blasphemers, a threat to Christendom.

My fellows in oppression, you who are treated as strangers in your own country, return to the Lord! You cannot effectively work and struggle for liberation if you are yourselves living in that which you are fighting. So come back to him who is the liberator of Israel. When he calls you to him, he doesn't do this so that he can store you up somewhere safe in heaven, but to liberate you and send you back with the word of truth to those powers from which you are liberated.

Stand by one another then, as children of the one mother and father. Serve God, as those women did, at the foot of the cross, and if it must be, to the grave. Never cease, by word and deed, to carry the gospel of liberation and reconciliation into the world, especially to those who oppress and persecute us. Fight this fight soberly, call upon God without ceasing.

For our fight is not against human foes, but against cosmic powers, against the authorities and potentates of this dark world, against the superhuman forces of evil in the heavens. Therefore take up God's armour; then you will be able to stand your ground when things are at their worst, to complete every task and still to stand. Stand firm, I say. Fasten on the belt of truth; for coat of mail put on integrity; let the shoes on your feet be the gospel of peace, to give you firm footing; and with all these, take up the great shield of faith, with which you will be able to quench all the flaming arrows of the evil one. Take salvation for helmet; for sword, take that which the spirit gives you — the words that come from God.

Psalm 1

Happy are those who reject the evil advice of tyrants,
who do not follow the example of sell-outs
and are not resigned to live as slaves.

Instead they find joy to be in God's commission
for the liberation of the oppressed,
and they work day and night without rest.

They are like trees that grow beside a stream,
that bear fruit at the right time,
and whose leaves do not dry up.
They succeed in everything they do.

But the traitors of the liberation cause are not
   like this;
they are like straw that the wind blows away.
Puppets in the hands of the oppressors
will be condemned by God.
They will have no share in the blessings of the Lord.

Those in God's service for the liberation of the downtrodden
are guided and protected by him.
But those who are instruments in the hands of the oppressors
are on the way to their doom.

Psalm 4

Answer me when I call unto you,
O God my advocate!
When they detained me, you helped me.
Remember me again and hear my prayer.

How long will you people insult us with the curse of apartheid?
How long will you trample on us?
While you are fondling your pets, you despise us.
How long will you refuse to accept
that we are all human beings?

Remember that the Lord will stop all this.
For we are not calling unto him only with words,
but also with our tears and blood,
yes, with our lives.

Tremble with fear and destroy all the evil laws;
think deeply of what you are doing now to us,
when you lie in silence in your beds.
Turn away from the demon of the "super race" to God
who in his love created all people equally.

There are many at this hour
who are screaming in pain and fear of death, O Lord;
Look on us as you looked on the oppressed in ages past.
Be our hope today and for years to come.

Be our guard in this time of trouble
and light with your presence the way to justice and peace.
The joy which you are giving to us
as we work and die for liberation,
is more than they will ever have in their affluence.

When I lie down in my shack
I go to sleep in peace;
you alone, O Lord, keep me perfectly safe.

Psalm 5

See my tears, O Lord,
and hear my sighs.
Listen to my screams for help,
my God and King!

I will never be tired to call unto you, O Lord,
you hear my voice in the morning
when I ask for guidance and protection in the new day.

You are never pleased with those who are doing wrong to their
    neighbours;
you allow no insult and oppression in your presence;
you cannot abide those who idolize their own race;
you hate apartheid.
You will destroy it with all its violent manifestations.

Your love gives us the strength and courage not to give up
    the process of breaking down the walls.
The love and fellowship of the believers is the foretaste
    of the life together in your kingdom.
Lord, keep me in this fellowship of those who do your will.
Strengthen me not to drop out of this way.

The enemies of your kingdom are telling many lies against your
    people.
The words in their newspapers and radios are flattering and
    smooth,
but full of deadly deceit.
But history is in your hands, O Lord,
and it will condemn and punish what they say and do;
their own plots will cause their ruin.

Protect those who love you;
so that they may be truly happy in their work for justice and
    peace.
Bless those who obey you,
and may your love protect them like a shield.

Psalm 6

Lord, do not be angry with me and rebuke me!
I am worn out by the terrible things which are taking place in
 our country;
give me strength, I am completely exhausted, physically and
 spiritually.
I am so troubled for I don't know what is being planned against
 me.
How long, O Lord, will you allow them to plot against us?

Come now, O Lord, before the execution of their evil plans;
in your mercy rescue us from their blood-stained hands.

I am worn out with grief when I think of what is happening in
 this country;
every night my bed is damp from my weeping;
my pillow is soaked with tears when I think of my children
who are growing up in this inhuman situation.
I can hardly see, my eyes are so swollen from the weeping
 over the suffering of my people.

The Lord hears my weeping;
he listens to the cry of the oppressed.
He will scatter all the enemies of justice and peace;
in sudden confusion they will be driven away.

Psalm 7

In this hour of despair and hopelessness
I come to you for comfort;
rescue me from my despair and give me faith, hope and love,
else I will be not able to participate in your saving work in the
    world;
I will from weariness collapse and die.

O Lord, my God, if I in my despair wronged anyone,
if I let a friend down or hurt in my impatience those who love
    me —
If I have done any of these things,
then do not leave me in my guilt to endless grief.
Forgive, O Lord, forgive me and restore me to your love.

Come in your love, O Lord our God;
come to us and strengthen the bond of love and fellowship
among all your people who work for righteousness and peace;
arise and help us!
Open the eyes and ears —
convert and convince with your Spirit
and with the examples of your true servants
those who have been misled by the promise of false justice and
    peace in this world.
Unite the people of the whole world in the spirit of your love,
and rule over us from above.
Judge in favour of the creation which you created in your love.
You looked at everything you had made and you were very
    pleased.
Therefore we pray unto you, O God,
have mercy on us and renew your creation.

I thank you, Lord, for I know that you are at work;
you hold the whole world in your hands and you can change it.
I will sing your praises at all times.

Psalm 23

The Lord is my shepherd;
I have everything I need.
He lets me see a country of justice and peace
and directs my steps towards his land.

He gives me new power.
He guides me in the paths of victory,
as he has promised.

Even if a full-scale violent confrontation breaks out
I will not be afraid, Lord,
if you are with me.
Your shepherd's power and love protect me.

You prepare for me my freedom,
where all my enemies can see it;
you welcome me as an honoured guest
and fill my cup with righteousness and peace.

I know that your goodness and love will
be with me all my life;
and your liberating love will be my home
as long as I live.

Psalm 27

The Lord is my light and my liberation;
I will fear no so-called world powers.
The Lord protects me from all danger;
I will never be afraid.

When their "security forces" attack me
and try to kill me,
they stumble and fall.
Even if their whole imperialist armies surround me,
I will not be afraid;
I will still trust in God my Liberator.

I have asked the Lord for one thing;
one thing only do I want:
to be his instrument in the struggle for liberation,
to be driven by his love.
In times of war he will shelter me;
he will keep me safe in his loving hands
and make me secure on a high rock.

So I will triumph over the oppressive regime.
With shouts of joy I will give my life
as a sacrifice in your service.
I will praise and sing freedom songs to my Lord.

Hear me, Lord, when I call to you!
Be merciful and answer me!
When you said "come and be my servant",
I answered, "I will come, Lord."
Do not hide yourself from me!

Do not be angry with me;
do not turn your servant away.
You have been my help;
do not leave me, do not abandon me,
O God, my Liberator.
My father and mother may abandon me,
but the Lord will be with me in this present situation and for
    ever.

Teach me, Lord, what you want me to do,
and lead me along in this difficult situation.
Do not abandon me to the worshippers of apartheid and their
    collaborators
who attack me with lies and threats.

I know that I will live to see in this present life
the Lord's victory over the enemies of the oppressed people in
    Southern Africa.
Trust in the Lord;
have faith, do not despair.
Trust in the Lord.

Psalm 33

All you who love righteousness and peace,
    shout with joy for what the Lord is doing;
    pray to him all you who trust in him,
    give thanks to the Lord with trumpets,
    sing to him with guitars.
Sing a song of victory to him;
    for what seems a dream, will soon be the reality —
    the Lord loves righteousness and peace.

The Lord frustrates the thoughts of those who conspire
    to postpone the day of our liberation;
    he prevents them from carrying out their evil plans.
But nobody can take away from his promises to us;
    no one will change or stop the plans of the Lord,
    for they endure for ever.

The Lord looks down from heaven
    and sees how they plot against justice and peace
    behind closed doors.
From where he rules, he looks down
    and sees the pain and the tears of the powerless.

Happy is the nation which does not forget him in its suffering.
Happy are the people for whom he is their God in the hour of
    darkness.

Their strength and victory
are gifts out of his hands,
for without God, our power will not liberate
    and our victory will be vain.

We put our hope in the Lord;
    he is our protector and our help.
We sing a song of victory to him;
    for with him in front of us,
    victory will be ours.

May your love fill our hearts,
    as we walk through the desert of hate and violence.
    Under your guidance we shall overcome.

Psalm 54

Save Africa by your power, O God;
set her free by your might.
Hear our prayer, O God;
listen to our words.

People who regard themselves as superior to us
are coming to attack us;
cruel men are killing our sons and daughters
and our old people —
men who call themselves Christians,
yet do not care about God.

But God is our helper;
the Lord is our defender;
he will destroy their evil plans because of his faithfulness.

I will gladly offer my life in your service
for the liberation of those who suffer.
I will give you thanks
because you are good.
You will rescue us from our troubles
and we will see our enemies defeated!

Psalm 55

Hear our prayer, O God;
do not turn away from our plea!
Listen to us and answer us;
Southern Africa is worn out by her worries.
She is terrified by the threats of her enemies,
crushed by the oppression of the wicked
who bring trouble on her.

We are terrified,
and the terrors of death crush us.
We are gripped by fear and trembling;
We are overcome with horror.
We wish we had wings like a dove,
to fly far away from the raging wind and storm.
O Lord, confuse the evil plans of our enemies!
There is violence and death in Namibia and South Africa;
the roads and towns are full of oppression,
    destruction and fraud.

But we call to the Lord God for help,
and he will liberate us.
Morning, noon and night
our groans go up to him,
and he will hear our voice.
He will bring us safely back
from the battles that we fight
against so many enemies.
God who has ruled from eternity
will hear us and defeat them;
for they refuse to change,
and they do not fear him.

O you people who suffer, trust in the Lord,
and he will defend you;
he will never let the oppressed be defeated.

But you, O God, will bring those murderers, liars and traitors
to their shame and defeat.
As for us, we will trust in you!

Psalm 62

I wait patiently for God to break the door
　　of this prison;
for there is nobody in this world who can help me.
God alone can help me not to be overpowered by fear;
　　He is at my side in this dark hour,
　　therefore I know that victory is mine.

Why all this huge military mobilization,
　　against those who do not even have a stick in their hands?
Why all these lies and cursing
　　against those who have no strength to defend themselves?

With my whole strength I cling to you,
　　you alone are my hope in this dark night;
　　you are on my side as I face this scorching heat of hate and
　　　　humiliation;
therefore I know that victory is mine.

My liberation and the restoration of my humanity
　　depend on God;
he is my lawyer in this situation
　　where I cannot defend myself.

Cling to him at all times, my people;
　　Share with him all the humiliation you suffer,
　　for he is our refuge and our strength.

Men, in their arrogance, present themselves as saviours
and think that they are almighty and everlasting.
　　But they are like a puff of breath;
　　they are lighter than a mere breath.

Do not put your trust in guns
　　for they are made by man.
Do not hope to gain righteousness and liberation
　　with unrighteousness and corruption;
　　for it will only lead you to defeat and shame.

When you feel strong, do not forget him who is on your side,
    for without him you are nothing.

For you yourself, O Lord, you will not be silent
until we have been saved on the new day, when
    humiliation will be no more.

Psalm 68

As smoke is blown away,
as wax melts in the fire,
so do racism, oppression and exploitation
perish in God's presence.
The oppressed and down-trodden are liberated in his presence;
they are happy and shout for joy.

God, who lives in slums and locations,
cares for orphans and protects widows.
He will give those who live outside in the cold
a home to live in,
and will lead those who dwell in the hell of apartheid
out into happy freedom.

O God, lead your people across the desert
of colonialism, oppression and racism.
Shake the foundations of the evil regime and destroy it.

May justice and peace rain on your people
and restore your worn-out land;
may the oppressed feel at home in their land,
and provide in your goodness for the exploited.

Praise the Lord, who weeps with us day after day;
he is the God who liberates us.
Our God is the Lord who rescues us from the opppressor.

O God, the march of the oppressed is seen by all,
and you are the king who leads us.
The singers of freedom songs are in front,
the music is the tears of the people,
and the blood of sons and daughters who die in the struggle.

Praise the Lord, children of Africa;
praise the Lord for ever and ever,
all you descendants of the oppressed!

Show your power, O God,
the power you have used on our behalf.
Rebuke the regime that works evil and destruction;

Rebuke those nations who supply it
with weapons to kill the people,
until they bow down before you and repent.

Sing to God, O children of Africa,
sing freedom songs to our Liberator.
Proclaim his power; his majesty is over the world,
his might is in the slums and locations.
He gives strength and power to the oppressed!

Psalm 69

Save us, O God!
We are sinking in deep mud,
and there is no solid ground;
we are out in deep water,
and the waves are about to wash us down.
We are worn out from calling for help,
and our throats are parched.
We strain our eyes,
looking for your help.

Those who hate us because of the colour of our skin
are more numerous than all the mountains and trees.
They are telling lies against us;
they are strong and want to destroy us;
they exploit our wealth day and night.

O Lord, do not let them destroy us,
do not let them deceive us.
It is because you made us black
that we are insulted,
that we are covered with shame.
We are like strangers in our own home,
like foreigners in our own land.

Our longing for liberation
burns in us like a fire;
the insults which are hurled at us fall on you,
because you made us.
We humble ourselves in prayer,
but the oppressors go on insulting us;
We put on clothes of mourning,
but the exploiters laugh at us.
They talk about us in the streets,
and sell-outs and puppets make up songs about us.

But as for us, we will call upon you, Lord;
answer us because of your great love,
because you keep your promise to liberate.
Save us from sinking in the mud of apartheid;
keep us safe from the enemies of freedom and peace;
and do not let the flood of oppression overpower us.

Lord, do not hide yourself from the oppressed;
we are in great trouble — answer us NOW!
Come to us and save us;
rescue us from our enemies.

When we are hungry, they give us poison;
when we are thirsty, they offer us vinegar.

Lift us out of our pain and despair;
O God, deliver us from oppression!
When the oppressed see it, they will be glad;
those who serve the Lord as servants of freedom and peace will
    rejoice.

The Lord listens to those in need, and does not
forget his people in prison.
Praise God, O you who suffer!
For to the oppressed and their descendants
will be restored their heritage.

Psalm 114

When the oppressed people left the house of colour
   worshippers,
when the despised left the state of slavery and racism,
they became the Lord's holy people,
the oppressed became his own possession.

The oppressors looked and ran away;
the worshippers of race and colour were paralyzed.

The mountains skipped like goats with joy;
and the hills jumped about like lambs in happiness.

Tremble, earth, at the coming of our Liberator,
at the presence of our God,
who hears the prayers of the poor,
who changes despair into hope and sorrow into joy!

Psalm 115

To you alone, O Lord our Liberator, to you alone
and not to us — whom you use as instruments of peace —
must glory be given, because of your constant love and faithful-
    ness,
because you oppose all powers of oppression.

Why should the nations ask us,
"Where is your Liberator?"
Our God goes ahead in our march of liberation;
he will free us from the yoke of bondage.

Their gods and liberators are luxury houses,
millions of Rands and expensive cars;
these are formed by human hands,
like the idols worshipped in ignorance.

The idols have mouths, but cannot speak,
and eyes, but cannot see.
They have ears, but cannot hear,
and noses, but cannot smell.
They have hands, but cannot feel,
and feet, but cannot walk;
they cannot make a sound.

All who believe and trust in them
become lifeless and inhuman like them.

Trust in the Lord, you oppressed people of the world;
he is fighting for you and he will protect you.
Trust in the Lord, you servants of God;
his help will never fail.
Trust in our Liberator, all you who follow him
in the struggle, and victory will be ours.

The Lord remembers us and will lead us;
he will bless the oppressed peoples
of the world and bring peace to all his servants.
He will bless everyone who follows him
through the dangerous battlefield,
the great and the small alike.

May the Lord give you courage and power,
you and your descendants!
May you be blessed by the Lord
who made heaven and earth!

Glory belongs to the Lord alone,
for he gives victory to us.
The Lord is not praised by traitors and cowards.
But we — his instruments in the liberation struggle
— will give thanks to him now and for ever.

Praise the Lord!

Psalm 121

I look up to the powerful of this world;
   will my help come from them?
My help comes from the Lord,
   who from my childhood
   took my weak hand in his strong hand
and led me in his way to this day.

He will not let me be unfaithful;
for he is always awake and will protect me.
Yes, my protector never sleeps,
he will guard me;
he is by my side to protect me from all dangers visible and
   invisible.
He will protect me from all dangers
as I go away and come back to my home;
in his strong hands I will be safe.
With this assurance and faith I will live and die.
Let the Lord's name be praised, now and for ever.

Psalm 126

When the day comes on which our victory
   will shine like a torch in the night,
   it will be like a dream.
We will laugh and sing for joy.
Then the other nations will say about us,
   "The Lord did great things for them."
Indeed, he is doing great things for us;
that is why we are happy in our suffering.

Lord, break the chains of humiliation and death,
   just as on that glorious morning
   when you were raised.
Let those who weep as they sow the seeds of justice and
   freedom,
gather the harvest of peace and reconciliation.

Those who weep as they go out as instruments of your love
   will come back singing with joy,
   as they will witness the disappearance of hate
and the manifestation of your love in your world.

Psalm 127

If the Lord does not build the nation,
the labour of those who build without him is fruitless.
   If the Lord does not lead us
   on the way to nationhood,
the nation will be without a future.
It will be of no avail to work for justice and freedom
      without him,
for then justice will turn into injustice
and liberation will become oppression.
But for those who trust in him and whom he loves,
   for them he will provide plentifully,
      even in their sleep.

Justice, freedom and peace will be the gifts from his loving
      hands
and they will never be corrupted or destroyed
   by the powers of evil.

Psalm 133

How wonderful it is, how pleasant,
to be healed of the corrosive disease of racism and separation;
and to live as God's people together in harmony.
The Spirit of the Lord will then fill the hearts
    and the minds of all the people.
Nobody will be judged any more on the basis of race or colour;
    but all will be ruled with justice and integrity.

The war will end and the people together will rebuild the
    country.
    There will be no reference to the colour of the skin,
    for all will be regarded as the people of God,
    the people he created in his image.
And this will be the beginning of what the Lord has promised —
    the life that never ends.

Psalm 137

By the rivers of foreign countries we sat down
    as refugees;
there we wept when we remembered the land
    of our birth.
We stopped singing our beloved songs
    of liberation.
Those who are helping our enemies wanted us to sing;
    they wanted us to entertain them:
"Sing us a song about the land whence you fled."

How can they expect us to entertain them
    with our suffering and tears?
May I never turn our struggle for freedom and peace
    into entertainment for those who are
    friends of our enemies!
May I never be able to sing again
    if I do not remember you,
    if I do not think of you,
    O country of my birth!

Remember, Lord, what the oppressors did
    the day they turned us into refugees.
Remember how they kept saying,
"Let us destroy them completely!"

You, enemies of freedom and peace,
    you will be discomfited.
Happy is the man who pays you back
    for what you have done to us —
who takes your rotten system of apartheid
    and smashes it against a rock.

Psalm 139

Lord, you have examined me and you know me.
You know everything I do;
from far away you understand all my thoughts.
You see me, whether I am confessing or denying you.
Even before I speak, you already know what I will say.
You are all around me on every side;
you protect me with your power.
Your knowledge of me is too deep,
for you knew me before I was born;
and this is beyond my understanding.

It is very dangerous to serve you in this world,
but where can I go
to escape from being the instrument of your peace?
What far place can I flee to, without confessing you?

If I withdraw myself into "neutrality",
   you would be there;
if I go into my office to hide behind my typewriter,
   you would be there;
if I take refuge in the farthest country away from the oppression
   of my people,
   you would be there, to remind me of what I promised you.
I could ask the darkness of my pain and humiliation
   to cover me,
or the light of your love in my life,
   to turn into darkness;
but even the night of my suffering dissolves in the light of your
   presence.

You created me in your image and loved me even before my
   mother conceived me.
I praise you,
what you do is so wonderful and above our human
   understanding.

Examine me, O God, and change my mind;
test me, and clean my thoughts.
Start the revolution in my life, create me anew,
and guide me in the everlasting way.

Towards a Confessing Church in Southern Africa

The church is the people on the way

The church of Jesus Christ is not a rigid national monument, which stands motionless in the middle of world events to maintain its status quo, but she is the body of the living Lord. She is visible. The Lord himself described her as the light which will lighten the world and as a city built on a hill to be seen by all. She is the nation of the new Exodus, on the way to meet her coming Lord. The path she takes does not lead through an invisible celestial world where justice, truth and love reign; it goes through this world where people despise, suppress and exploit one another. But it is not a way of defeat; it is the way of the victory which has been accomplished by her Lord.

The church does not walk her way in silence or "neutrality", but she sings with a clear voice the song of victory and liberation. A hymn that shakes the evil powers and pulls down all destructive schemes and ideologies. A hymn that lifts up the oppressed, poor and despised people from the dust and brings down the proud and mighty from their thrones. A hymn that calls the whole universe to Jesus Christ. The church has not been called to spend herself in a flood of irrelevant words, but to a powerful witness and service which leads to revolutionary renewal for those who will listen and surrender themselves to Jesus Christ. The words of J.H. Oldham are still a powerful challenge to Christians in a situation of racism and separation:

> Christianity is not primarily a philosophy but a crusade. As Christ was sent by the Father, so he sends his disciples to set up in the world the kingdom of God. His coming was a declaration of war — a war to the death against the powers of darkness. He was manifested to destroy the works of the devil. Hence when Christians find in the world a state of things that is not in accord with the truth which they have learned from Christ, their concern is not that it should be explained but that it should be ended. In that temper we must approach everything in the relations between races that cannot be reconciled with the Christian ideal.

The vocabulary of God versus the vocabulary of evil structures

The prophetic voice of the church does not use the vocabulary of this world but of God who is the giver of the message. Where a messenger makes use of the vocabulary of this world, the message becomes a mere repetition of what the world is proclaiming. Such a message is a lie; if it is carried in the name of God, the messenger is a false prophet.

The true prophet of the Lord sees and judges the situation and the events in this world, not by the criteria laid by this world, but on the basis of God's word. That is the word of truth, justice and love.

The prophet Amos is a clear example of this. He preached to the people of the Northern Kingdom, at a time of great material prosperity but spiritual poverty. Through the eyes of prophecy, Amos could see the injustice in this prosperity which was limited to the rich and based on the oppression of the poor. Peace and justice were empty slogans. Their religion was godless like the Christless Christianity of many "Christian" countries.

We see in the prophecy of Amos and the other prophets the confrontation between the vocabulary of God and that of the world. The messengers of the world said that there was prosperity and peace, and boasted about it. The prophetic voice answered that there was no real prosperity and peace, only a situation of exploitation and the complete absence of peace. The world boasted about its religion as many today are boasting about the "Christian" South Africa and the "Christian" Western civilization, which must be protected by all means. The prophetic voice says that God hates all "worship" which ignores the evil and acquiesces in oppression. God cannot stand the worship which is deaf to the cries of agony in this world and blind to the suffering of humanity. In the Southern African situation, God hates the Christless "Christianity", in which the Holy Trinity has been made subordinate to race, colour and a tradition of conquest. God will not accept the prayers and hymns offered by the powerful in places where many people are being excluded because of their race and the colour of their skins. If the book of the prophet Amos were not a part of the Bible, it would have been banned in South Africa!

> The Sovereign Lord says, people of Israel, go to the holy place in Bethel and sin if you must. Go to Gilgal and sin with all your might. Go ahead and bring animals to be sacrificed morning after morning, and bring your tithes every third day. Go ahead, and offer your bread in thanksgiving to God, and boast about the extra offerings you bring. This is the kind of thing you love to do...

> You people hate anyone who challenges injustice and speaks the
> whole truth in the court. You have oppressed the poor and robbed
> them of their grain. And so you will not live in the fine stone houses
> you build or drink wine from the beautiful vineyards you plant. I
> know how terrible your sins are and how many crimes you have
> committed. You persecute good men, take bribes, and prevent the
> poor from getting justice in the courts. And so, keeping quiet in
> such evil times is the clever thing to do...
> The Lord says, I hate your religious festivals: I cannot stand
> them. When you bring me burnt-offerings and grain-offerings, I
> will not accept the animals you have fattened to bring me as
> offerings: I do not want to listen to your harps. Instead, let justice
> flow like a stream, and righteousness like a river that never goes dry
> (Amos 4:4-5; 5:10-13, 21-24).

The messengers of this world said that they were protecting
"law and order", but the prophetic voice says that this is only
protection of injustice and brutal oppression. There are many
voices within the church of Jesus Christ. The voices of false
prophets call the church to adapt herself to the evil conditions in
this world. Many Christians do this, and regard it as the normal
way of Christian living. They go even further, and preach that
obedience to God demands such accommodation to the structures of the world.

> In order to fulfill our Christian responsibility in a multiracial
> country, we have to be subject to the recognized guiding principles
> (i.e. the constitution of the land) of the country. Any faction which
> opposes this, must take to the catacombs.

This is only one example of the way Christians provide a
religious basis for the apartheid system in Southern Africa.
When the messengers begin to benefit from unjust and oppressive structures they adapt themselves to them and forget their
calling. This was the problem Amaziah had with Amos.
Amaziah and the kings prospered from a system in which people
were exploited and oppressed. But the prophetic voice of Amos
denounced this system and boldly proclaimed that it was
doomed to destruction. The interests of the priest Amaziah and
the king Jeroboam were now in danger, and that was why
Amaziah tried to silence the voice of Amos.

But here there is no room for compromise with the evil
powers of our day. We must instead make a critical examination

of the existing situation and search for God's will for the whole of humankind:

> So then, my brothers, because of God's great mercy to us I appeal to you: Offer yourselves as a living sacrifice to God, dedicated to his service and pleasing to him. This is the true worship that you should offer. Do not conform yourselves to the standards of this world, but let God transform you inwardly by a complete change of your mind. Then you will be able to know the will of God — what is good and is pleasing to him and is perfect (Rom. 12:1-2).

"How I wish you were either one or the other"

A prophetic voice can never be neutral in a situation of conflict. Neutrality has in fact no place in the vocabulary of God. There is and will be no occasion when the prophetic voice can be tamed into neutrality. How can the messenger of God be neutral, while the God who is sending him or her is never neutral? This is the dilemma of many Christians all over the world, but particularly in Southern Africa. Apart from the very few voices of confessing men and women, here prevails a silence which is putting the credibility of the church at stake. While Christians in many parts of the world are shedding tears in solidarity with us, the prophetic voices in our countries are muted. It is as if there were nothing wrong.

Another problem of the church in Southern Africa, which is yet another obstacle in the way of a courageous and unambiguous confession and service, is the fact that people with different messages, which are in conflict with one another, pretend to be sisters and brothers with one single message. For the sake of a sham unity, confrontation is always avoided, and the message loses its strength and credibility in this process. Time is running out, and people stand in need of an urgent, clear and unambiguous voice.

The messenger must not proclaim the message with words only but with his or her whole life as a member of the community of which he or she is a part. This is the problem of many Christians in South Africa, that in many ways the message which they are preaching, singing and praying has little to do with their daily life.

On Sunday they confess: "There is one Shepherd and one flock, one baptism and one Church." And then they go and live in a situation of double separation on the basis of race and denomination, without any qualms. That kind of message is devoid of all credibility and it makes the messengers themselves liars in the eyes of the world. But the most tragic and frightening thing is that by doing this, they make the Holy One who sends them a liar as well.

The church has placed herself under the judgment of God. It will not benefit the church if she, in a spirit of self-righteousness, abuses and condemns the revolutions of our time; it will be much better if she sees in her suffering God's judgment, and the call for repentance and faithfulness. In that painful moment she will experience anew that God remains faithful to the old promises:

> Afterwards I will pour out my spirit on everyone: your sons and daughters will proclaim the message: your old men will have dreams and your young men will see visions (Joel 2:28).

That message was not given to be confined to conference halls and nicely worded resolutions. It was not meant to be taken out of the realities of this world and to be preached in a vacuum. The great commission was that the good news must be taken to all peoples everywhere. It is not to be whispered in ambiguous terms, but to be proclaimed boldly and in its entirety, in the streets and in the market places.

The denial of the good news in South Africa and Namibia

The way of life in South Africa and Namibia, based on the policy of apartheid, is directly opposed to the good news that God through Christ has removed the walls of separation between himself and human persons and between human persons.

> Racism is a blatant denial of the Christian faith. It denies the effectiveness of the reconciling work of Jesus Christ... through whose love all human diversities lose their significance; it denies our common humanity in the creation and our belief that all men are made in God's image; it falsely asserts that we find our significance in terms of racial identity rather than in Jesus Christ.

The "good news" which is proclaimed by the laws of the land and protected by the huge army, builds walls of separation that lead to alienation, suspicion and hatred. The differences of nationalities, languages and cultures, which are the gifts of God to enrich humanity, are used by the apartheid regime as bricks to build walls of division between races and people. Our fellowship one with another is based on the liberating gospel of Jesus Christ. It is in the Bible that we learn that we are all of us created in the image of God, and that we have all been redeemed by Christ. But this good news violates the law of our land. Here we have other gods — race, colour and tradition. These three gods determine the whole way of life in South Africa and Namibia. They are in the eyes of the state far more important than the Holy Trinity!

These three gods determine where I should feel at home; where I should relax or not; in which vehicle I should travel and which seat I should occupy in that vehicle; whom I should love; what kind of education I should receive and where I should get medical care; where I should worship and even where I should be buried. Whatever I think, speak or do, should be for the honour and glory of race, colour and tradition.

And all this is based on a grievously distorted biblical interpretation. Anyone who dares to oppose this "divine" system, is jailed and tortured, or deported, or murdered. Those who benefit from this evil system, because of their race and the colour of their skins, regard it as the greatest responsibility laid on them by their "Christian faith" to protect it. They believe that their whole existence depends on that.

In the South African and Namibian context you are a good person and a believer if you support this system; but when you oppose it, you become a danger to society and an unbeliever.

"The Southern African Council of Churches was using funds obtained from overseas to launch and support actions and activities which were in no way different from those of the African National Congress," the Minister of Law and Order, Mr Louis Le Grange, said the other day.

Speaking during the debate on his budget vote he said that in the majority of cases the Council's actions and activities were closely related to and synchronized with those of the ANC:

> Despite never having uttered a word of criticism about the activities of the ANC and refusing his Council permission to visit

the operational area where black and white South Africans were defending their country, Bishop Tutu seemed to find it strange that he should be accused of harbouring pro-ANC sympathies.

By the promotion of his and his Council's activities, certain aims and objects of the ANC were also promoted.

The funds used by the SACC to launch and support actions and activities which are nowhere different from those of the ANC, and in fact in the majority of cases are closely related to and in fact synchronized with those of the ANC, emanate mainly from two sources: Scandinavian government agency sources, sources such as the World Council of Churches and other religious groups, from the World University Service and similar groups. All having a common aim — *the destruction of South Africa*.

Responsible members of member churches must now seriously ask themselves for how long they are prepared to entertain and accept the fact that the secretary of the SACC and/or the body as such, favours and/or supports subversive elements and encourages the build-up of a revolutionary climate in South Africa.

"The government is finding it increasingly difficult to accept this situation any longer," he said.

What they refuse to see is that the enemies of South Africa are not those who fight apartheid; apartheid itself, with all its demonic manifestations, is the real enemy of South Africa, and the destruction of that evil will be the salvation of all the people in South Africa.

Allan Boesak's open letter to Desmond Tutu is a prophetic voice which must be heeded:

My first reaction was anger. What utter rubbish, I thought. Precisely who is the danger to our society and to the future of this country? Who has caused the problem that now plagues South Africa? Who has taken away the few pitiful political rights that we had so that they could inflict their policies upon us without responsibility to us? Whose laws are making criminals out of men, women and children who want only a decent life together with a family? Whose greed and avarice claim 87% of the land and in so doing rob millions of South Africans of their birthright? Who is trampling on our God-given dignity?

Not by any stretch of the imagination can you be accused of "creating a revolutionary climate" in South Africa. No, it is your very accusers who, through their intransigence and their stubborn refusal to respect the dignity of black personhood, are doing that. It is they who are denying us meaningful participation, insulting us with the puppet institutions they themselves would have scorned. It is they who through their draconian measures, setting aside the rule of law, have banned organizations that wanted peaceful change, detained without trial, banned and exiled the best of the sons and daughters of South Africa.

It is they who have done so much to help convince generations of black South Africans that non-violent protest has no chance in South Africa. For years we have petitioned, marched, pleaded, cried, tried to speak to the conscience of white South Africa's government. They have answered with police, with detentions and teargas, with dogs and guns. And with that infinite contempt of violent men who have nothing left but the power of the gun. No, it is not you who have turned so many of our old people into creatures without hope and joy and so many of our young people into desperadoes. It is they.

You are a man in deep love with your country. But they will never understand that. For them, loving South Africa means to accept apartheid and white supremacy, humiliation and exploitation. It means to bow your head in submission and say "Ja Baas" even if deep in your heart you despise apartheid and all that system has made of all of us, white and black. It is to fight for a country where we shall no longer be ruled by fear and greed. But you speak a truth that is too humbling, a message that is too disturbing. The love you offer your country is too demanding, and in a real sense, too overwhelming. It is true that a prophet is not honoured or loved in his own land, but it is also true that a nation that cannot respond to such a love has set fire to its own future.

So let them accuse you, millions of us love and support you. Let them accuse you; when the true history of this country comes to be written, you will be counted as a true son who fought for her integrity and her life. Let them accuse you, in the church of Christ you should be honoured as a pastor, a prophet whose obedience to God was more than the fear for those who rule this world. Let them accuse you; in that Great Day he will call you a good and faithful servant. For I affirm with all my heart the words of the Belgic Confession, that on that day "the faithful and elect shall be crowned with glory and honour... all tears shall be wiped from their eyes; and their case which is now condemned by many judges and magistrates as heretical and impious will then be known to be the case of the Son of God."

The true discipleship and the cross of victory

Yes, many are silent because they fear for their lives. This fear turns them into false prophets. They try vigorously to

develop a kind of theology which will never bring them in
confrontation with the rulers of this world. They become hypo-
crites, collaborators and liars in the eyes of the Lord and the
suffering people in the world. Not somebody from outside, but
these false prophets of today — and they are many — are the
real enemies of the church of Jesus Christ, because of their
distortion of the message of liberation.

In Matthew 3:1-12, we see the living example of a very
humble man who did not fear to stand alone, not only in the
Judean desert, but also in the desert of injustices, hatred and
separatedness.

The detailed description of John's clothes is deliberate, for it
takes us in our spirit back to one of the greatest prophets in the
history of Israel, the prophet Elijah who, in obedience to the
Lord, shook the foundations of Israel's godless religion and
self-confidence (2 Kings 1:2-18).

By involving Elijah in his narrative, the evangelist says: The
same Yahwe who sent Elijah is the one who is sending John.
With the same word and purpose: to plant and to pull out; to
break down and to build up; to throw away and to gather; to kill
and to raise. The words of our Lord Jesus Christ addressed to
the crowds point to the life of the man who has devoted himself
utterly to the cause of the Son of God:

> While John's disciples were leaving, Jesus spoke about him to
> the crowds: "When you went out to John in the desert, what did you
> expect to see? A man dressed up in fancy clothes? People who dress
> like that live in palaces. Tell me, what did you go out to see? A
> prophet? Yes, indeed, but you saw much more than a prophet. For
> John is the one of whom the scripture says: 'God said, I will send
> my messenger ahead of you to open the way for you'" (Matt. 11:
> 7-10).

Martin Luther King was one who witnessed in the tradition of
John the Baptist:

> If a man is 36 years old, as I happen to be, and some great truth
> stands before the door of his life, some great opportunity to stand
> up for that which is right and that which is just, and he refuses to
> stand up because he wants to live a little longer and he is afraid his
> home will get bombed, or he is afraid that he will lose his job, or he
> is afraid that he will get shot... he may go on and live until he is 80,

and the cessation of breathing in his life is merely the belated announcement of an earlier death of the spirit.

Indeed a man dies when he refuses to stand up for that which is right. A man dies when he refuses to take a stand for that which is true.

John was arrested and put in prison. After a certain period in prison, his head was cut off and given as a "gift" to Herodia's daughter, on her mother's cruel advice. Out of fear, many Christians find it wiser to keep silent in the apartheid situation.

John was commissioned to prepare in the wilderness a road for the Lord. This was — and is — not an easy task. It is easier to construct a road in the Namibia desert than in the wilderness of apartheid, alienation and animosity, the wilderness of war and death.

Those who are preparing the way in such a desert must know that they will be hurt, even killed. But the Lord in whose service they are "will be with them all the days, unto the end of the world", and he will give them everlasting life as the price of victory.

Their voices will be heard by all generations and will never die. That is why these words sound as fresh now as when they were first uttered:

> Why do we fear the fury of the world powers? Why don't we take the power from them and give it back to Christ? We can still do it today... We can send out to all believers this radical call to peace. The nations are waiting for it in the East and in the West... Shall we desert the individuals who are risking their lives for this message? The hour is late... and dreadful is the distrust which looks out of all men's eyes. The trumpets of war may blow tomorrow. For what are we waiting? Do we want to become involved in this guilt as never before? We want to give the world a whole word — a courageous word, a Christian word. We want to pray that this word may be given us today. Who knows if we shall see each other again another year?

During the church struggle before the second world war, the overwhelming majority of church leaders in Germany hoped that by making concessions they would buy the freedom of their churches from the pressure of the dictatorship. They were more concerned about their day-to-day administrative problems, finances and the construction of new church buildings.

They thought that through private discussions of their problems with the dictator they could guarantee a measure of security. This was a grave miscalculation. What Irenaeus said is still true today: "The seed of the church is the blood of the martyrs." The dictatorship which the church had not challenged took its silence for weakness and intensified its pressure. The church became a tool in the hands of ideologies.

It is frightening to see how this situation is repeating itself in Southern Africa. John confronted the Jewish spiritual leadership in public and called them to repentance. He told them bluntly that they would not escape the punishment of God if they did not change their ways. If he were living today, he would have been excommunicated, and jailed or hanged by the dictatorships of our times.

O Lord, what do you want me to do?

The axe is already at the root of the evil system. The suffering people are waiting with tears of hope for the voice of comfort. Who is going to tell them that they have suffered long enough?

The nation is on the verge of devastation, and there may well erupt a full-scale war. Southern Africa needs a voice which will call her back from this impending destruction. But in Christ the lesser loyalties for nation and race should make way for the greater loyalty to the kingdom of God. If there is one message which Pentecost brings home, it is that of the fundamental difference between a system of separation and Christianity.

Apartheid by its very nature divides and destroys: Christianity unites and gives new life. Apartheid inevitably forces people of different tribes and cultures apart and thereby creates hostility and enmity. Jesus Christ is the life of the world and he calls and sends his church to be engaged in apostolic service for the suffering and the poor of this world, and to proclaim with faithfulness the good news of love to all people everywhere, to the ends of the earth and to the end of time.

The first step towards a radical change in our life as Christians in Southern Africa is the confession of our sins, the sorrowful acknowledgment that in our divisions along racial, ethnic and denominational lines we do not manifest the reality of the church of Jesus Christ. This confession can and will be meaningful only if it is lived in the life of the congregations and of society as a whole. This means a concerted resistance, an open disobedience of all those laws which violate and deny the dignity and equality of all human beings.

Christians, in spite of all their weakness, are still parts of the body of Christ, and the Lord and Head of the church, in his love and mercy, is both able and willing to do great things through them for the wellbeing of humanity and the manifestation of his kingdom here and now.

They must come together across the boundaries of denominations and race, to work for the elimination of injustice, poverty, illiteracy and underdevelopment.

All members of congregations from the different denominations must put pressure on their leaders to accept the recovery of the visible unity of the church of Christ as a top priority in prayer and Christian action. Together with their leaders, they must seek new opportunities for service and proclamation.

Exchange of pulpits between the denominations must be accepted by all Christians as normal practice, for single acts of worship or for longer periods.

Meetings between young and old, women and men, for fellowship and for the frank exchange of views must be a part of the normal practice of all Christians from different denominations and races.

All theological training should be genuinely ecumenical and non-racial.

In their struggle for liberation, all Christians must stand together in breaking down divisive ethnic barriers to promote the unity of the oppressed in Southern Africa.

I conclude these few words with a word from a man who will be remembered as a prophet and pastor in the confessing church in Southern Africa:

> With Pentecost a new day dawned in history, never experienced before, bringing about the formation of a new community called the church. Through the outpouring of the Holy Spirit a number of people, the majority of whom were Jews by birth (and the remainder Jews by adoption) from a number of nations, were fused together into a new, all-inclusive fellowship of love which, by its very nature, challenged every convert's loyalty to all other existing fellowships. Christ has already previously predicted the nature of the choice which people would have to make by indicating the

demand which discipleship and the following of Christ would make when he had said: "If anyone comes to me and does not hate his own father and mother and wife and children and brothers and sisters, yes, and even his own life, he cannot be my disciple" (Luke 14:26). Here in Pentecost then is created the fellowship of a common celebration with infectious joy and happiness, a common mission.